Poems from the Cradle of Dreams

Also by Catharine Steinberg and published by Ginninderra Press
Signs of a Poetic Life

Catharine Steinberg

Poems from the Cradle of Dreams

Acknowledgements

I wish to thank Stephen Matthews and Brenda Eldridge of Ginninderra Press for their encouragement of Australian poets country wide, and in accepting my second book of poems for publication, *Poems from the Cradle of Dreams*.

I wish to also thank them for publishing my first book of poems titled *Signs of a Poetic Life* in 2017. One of my poems 'The Mountains Song' appears in *Wild*, an anthology edited by Joan Fenney and published in 2018 by Ginninderra Press on the anniversary of their tenth year as a publishing company in Port Adelaide.

Without Ginninderra Press, my poems would still be potential seeds hidden and forgotten inside closed folders and lifeless drawers.

Thank you.

This book is dedicated to my mother

Poems From the Cradle of Dreams
ISBN 978 1 76041 752 9
Copyright © text Catharine Steinberg 2019
Cover photo: Catharine Steinberg

First published 2019 by
Ginninderra Press
PO Box 3461 Port Adelaide 5015 Australia
www.ginninderrapress.com.au

Contents

The Crucible	7
I Shall Listen	8
Tiptoeing Seagulls	9
Will You Remember?	11
Seeking Harmony Again	13
Fragments of the Self	14
A Song of Hope at Singularity	15
Night Flight (Dream)	17
Running out of air	18
White Feather of No Surrender	20
Natures Run	21
Distant Thunder	23
My Little Shadow	24
Let's run away	25
Loss of the Sound of the Sea	26
Falcon	28
Bushland Folk	30
Hold on!	32
Fish in the wrong sea	33
Ode to the Rambling House	34
Blown Away	35
Between the lines	36
Unpredictable Weather	37
February in Sydney	39
The Pointless Point	40
Fun at the Very Expensive Sydney Hotel	42
African Tapestry	44
The Harmless Man	46
Life at Traffic Lights	48
A Painful Etching	49

Incongruity	53
Camp Figtree	56
The Goodbye Tale	58
The Frogs Dream	60
Images of Tsunamis and Bubbles	61
Disturbances	63
Long Lost, Last Deeplove	64
The Thing in Itself	66
A Force of Nature	68
Below 432 Hertz	70
Mass Extinctions	72
Free Fall	73
Farewell Messages	75
The Gaps	76
Another Day in Finality	78
Walking in the Park	80
Water	82
Water Colours	83
Selective Memories	85
Ordinary Things	87
Humming	88
Dear Old Soul	89
Angel Wings	90
Ferryman from the River Styx	92
Rose Water	94
Not Ever	95
Green sky	96
Dear You	97
In the moment	98
Thanking God	100
The Muse Slumbers	102
The Blackbird	103

The Crucible

The birth of poetry
Lies in a cradle of dreams.
And it is here in the Crucible
Where life takes on many forms.

On one side of birth
There an infinite fertile field
Where thoughts grow and flourish
Like seedlings in the soul.

On the other side
Any gardener can tell you
About the deep desire for life.
That she is not afraid
To nurture into finite existence
With her humble trowel and shovel,
The seeds that have been scattered
To her out of the vastness.
And to delight in the fruits of her labour
For an instant.

We know that a thin blue line
Is the only track in which life
Lives out the poetry of its dreams
On this planet.

And that the infinite of the universe
Evolves itself into thinking thoughts
In the Crucible.
In this earthly time and place.

And then wonders… Why?

I Shall Listen

I shall listen to the rampant birdsong
As I dive below the litter of wasted leaves
To reach the place of rambling roses.
Where nasturtiums bob their yellow heads
In the sunny warmth of intense pleasures
That only living things feel, without memory.

I shall listen to the early morning quiet
And the solitude of trees and stones
As the day finds itself waking into life.
As the crickets tune their violins
And cloudy shadows play hide and seek
Across the baby pink sky.

I shall listen as butcher birds duet
And cleanse away the long dark sorrows
That clog up vital streams
That flow from the mysteries of the soul.
To pull apart the shades of night
And sing the morning chorus of delights.

And I shall listen to the listening
As I climb up back up through the noisy day.
And clasp close to me the precious poems
That have arrived like birthday packages
With the messenger who calls at midnight.
Gifts found by chance in the toy box
Of morning consolations.

And I shall listen…

Tiptoeing Seagulls

Seagulls tiptoe above the incoming tide.
Grey and white feathers blown carelessly aside.
They run and flap, dip and glide.

Dancing in a time capsule.

We also wander.
Altogether along the sand.
Solidly like gentle giants caught up in the foam.

White clouds build at the edge of the sky.
Like snowy peaks that lace over sea and land.
Our home.

Dreaming quietly of farms and mountains
We walk and sometimes talk.
Our voices drowned by the ceaseless sound
Of the shimmering ocean.

A world away in our hearts
After long separations.

Only to leave again like the outgoing tide.

The seagulls run on tiptoes
Dancing before us.
Busy.

Catching mementos.

And gliding over the windswept spray
With ruffled feathers
They tiptoe away
Leaving tiny footprints in their wake.

On a perfectly captured blue and white day.

Will You Remember?

Will you remember
The winnowing voice
In the secret passageways
That led to the Royal Highway
Of our dreams? *

Or will the tunnels of time
Disremember the truth
In the conversations
Of a faithful heartbeat
That united the mind
To a still quiet place?

Will all of creation
And what is precious
Be lost to you
In the storms of life?

Where souls are washed
Up on foreign beaches
And where the shipwreck
Of grand desires
Plummets to the depth
Of the deepest abyss?

Can you still find your way back
Under the weight
Of the gravity of suffering
And all that you carry about you,
To the refuge of the island's shore?

And where long ago
You once felt complete,
Will you listen again
In an open wondering way
To imperceptible murmurings
In the deepest knowledge
Of your being?

* 'Dreams are the royal road to the unconscious.' Sigmund Freud

Seeking Harmony Again

It was harmonious, once.
Then a musical note was lost,
Then another, and another.
Like petals dropping from a flower.
Now the tune is not melodious
But a cacophony of jarring notes
That screech and jostle
For their place on life's stage.*

I seek Harmony again
For the perfect pitch that was lost,
In the quality of tone now forgotten
The vibration of a single pure note.
A merging of all things, and nothing.

---

*'All the world's a stage.' *As You Like It*, William Shakespeare

Fragments of the Self

The palest whiff

Of shredded remnants castes about,
Like a soul lost at sea.
A stifled hurt
That cannot, will not,
Mend itself.

The days grow in number
From the past,
The future's short.
The present has no time

And cannot, will not
Capture.

I try to run

To keep up
To stay ahead of myself.
And yet I stand so still.
I want to find a self.
The fragment that was lost.
But cannot, will not
Stay to care for me.

And other complexities

Scoff and cruelly wound.
And all the while

Patience stands quietly by,
Listening to all the fragments
With a true heart.

A Song of Hope at Singularity

On a sea of infinity
I float like a singular dot
Washed away by the tide.

The waves to my present
Meet now here through me
And drift to the event horizon
Of possibilities and receding
Future recollections.

Past and future combine
As bubbles,
That storm timelessly
In their corner
Of the multiverse.

Then slip away
Quietly
To another dimension
As if nothing has happened
At all.

I am at the centre
Of my known universe
Where else should I be?

And in truth there is no proof
Of anything or anyone at all
Existing anywhere
At any time.

Only here where I live
Am I present with me
In the fluctuating
Moment of change.

And my hope is that you,
Who now seem to be nowhere,
Still live somewhere
Close by me.

In a field overflowing
With the flowers
Of our memories and dreams.

Night Flight (Dream)

They say she must flee from the light of reality.
And I am the one who should guide her.

They say they'll catch up with their torches and cars.
And I know they intend to be kind.

But she asks me to hurry to run faster and faster.
As we stumble away in the dark.

I carry a gold watch that flickers with time.
Casting flashes of light on the track.

I have to find faith and a sense of what's right.
For the girl who is weeping and clings to my back as we run.

We ride the wild ponies that appear from the void.
And their hooves drum like thunder
As I clutch a white mane in my hand.

We gallop without light and are blinded throughout
By the endless black shadows of night.

I'm never afraid though her weeping overwhelms
The silence of dark that surrounds us.

At last we arrive through a hole in the dream
Where candles glow softly and folks gather round like ghosts.

I lay her still weeping in the arms of another
Who will love her forever.
Only then can we rest from the flight.

Running out of air

Step inside the envelope
Through the door of change.
The sunken treasure
Is visited by shafts of light.

A small bird sings
Himself to pieces
In the hovering air above.

Moments of change
Have been heralded
And time flips over
The wave that delights in its curve
As dolphins chase the surf.

A storm far out to sea
Only hears its own lonely roaring
To the heaving ocean
At midnight.
Even the wind sighs in its sleep.

Time lapses into spider threads
That dangle me to the new horizon.
While I, a watchful eye
On hopefulness, do keep.

But I grow tired
Of being in this swamp.
A relentless ecosystem
Of no freedom from myself.

The restlessness
Of deeper turmoil
Bubbles in old despairing sinkholes.

The tunnelled light to hope
Seems hard to reach.
And I'm running out of air.

White Feather of No Surrender

We are clinging to a raft
Of desires.
A large white feather
Afloat on a lagoon.

This time
There is no surrender.

Light as air, it is a lifeboat
To the future.
An object of flight
That carries us
Over the watery expanse
To secrets in our hearts.

Every day is a history book
Of empires vast and small
That rise and fall.

But we seek the truth that lives
Between the floating dreams.

Nature's Run

In the soft flesh of morning
An intense wish to gallop
Builds up like a passion
For sunbeams.

And like runaway horses
Flying over green pastures,
They run down the tracks
Where pretty weeds dance
And wild flowers still drench in the dew.

Where insects and worms
Delve deep in the soil,
They delight the dank corners
And tangles of roots with moist light.

Then zoom through branches
While leaves wave about,
Wanting to join in the play.

Where creatures and birds,
Lie hidden all day
And watch very quietly till night.

Hot fiery steeds speed up at high noon
Gamboling over soft petals.
That reveal their sweet secrets
In shadowy wombs
With a quiver and shiver to bees.

The air smells of honey
And fresh like new tadpoles
That wriggle and squiggle in rivers.

Where trouts wrestle and leap
To catch insects that buzz
Under the cool forest trees.

Times rippling expanse
Contracts like an ocean
Around whales and tiny seahorses.
That dive deep like blue swallows
Into lengthening yellow light.

Thousands of bats shimmy,
Flap and fly up.
Their pitched squeaks alive in the canopy.
That flows like a cup from green into orange
And deepens to a red glowing sky.

The shy mother of moons
Sails up on her swing
Over the arc of horizons.

She blossoms anew to a darkening hue
And gives birth to star children
In an ancient celestial dance.

At the twilight of glory
She calls for gold horses
From the purse of her spangled dreams.

And as she kisses the sunset
A loving goodbye
She gallops up to the glistening stream.

Distant Thunder

There's a sound of distant thunder
Heavy roll of bowling balls.
Clatter of a child's marbles
Flung forcefully on the floor.

Blobs of rain like molten glass
Crash miraculously on the ground.
A thousand rainbow colours
And all around sound.

A child's heavenly collection
Of amazing marble showers.
On it goes, on and on
Rollicking through endless hours.

Loud barrage of noise
Fantastic prisms of light.
Cacophony enough,
To delight the heart of any fearless child.

My Little Shadow

My little shadow follows me round and round
Hippity hoppity over the ground.
Whenever I turn to see if he's there
He imitates me and then leaps in the air.

I've tried to run away into the sun
But he elongates from where we'd begun.
At night he swamps me completely in dark
I wish I had got rid of him from the start.

I should secretly snip him from off my feet
Roll him up and hid him somewhere deep.
But then I'd miss him and think he's sad
Not to be jumping about and driving me mad.

Let's run away

Yes!
Run away with me
Run, run away
Lets run.

Far from angry faces
Let's run away from pain.
From tempests and from storms
Let's run to far-off places.

You and me
Yes!
Let's run.

Away to mountain tops
Let's run and jump in rivers
And dream on downy pillows.
Let's run till we're boiling hot.

Yes!
Run away with me
Run, run away
Let's run.

You and me.
Yes!
Let's run.

Loss of the Sound of the Sea

On sleepless nights such as this
When holidays have run
Their course and oceans roar
And stars riot overhead,
I mourn for the loss
Of the sound of the sea.

My breath feels gone
Like a fish out of water
My heart aches in a vice.
As though it could break.

I wonder how long it will be
Before I'm back here again with thee.
When will I hear
The stories you tell
Of the deep blue yonder?

When will the links to the past
Of dreamy sea gardens
Be seen again
Through your eyes?
And when will you sing to me
Safe in our haven
Away from the harrowing storms?

I want to be free
To soar like the sea eagle
Who searches me out
With her soul piercing eyes
As she circles around in the sky.

I wish to fly to great heights
Like that bird with you,
Dive to great depths
Like that fish with you.
And never wake up
Away from you
To the harsh bite of life.

But the day slowly wakes
To a grey old world,
Where I'm tied
Tightly down
To the infinite gravity
Of ground.

And I feel like the mermaid
Who has lost her voice and her tail
All for the love of…
Well!
I have to wonder for what?

Dawn finally comes.
The wind has died down,
The tide has turned back.
The sound of the sea has gone.

You have gone.

Falcon

A falcon soars over a crevasse
Lifted by thermal undercurrents
Bridging the void
Of hungry non-survival.
Climbing to a great height
He sees with piercing eyes
Small movements of prey below.

Spiralling downwards
He gently folds his wings
And plummets vertically
Earthwards like a bullet.
Only the rustling sound
Of icy wind
Through his feathered down
Betrays murder in his breast.

Down and down.
Straight and silent
Like an arrow
Finding its mark.
And just as sudden
Spreads his wings.
Talons now bared
In final descent.
He swoops down with a rush
And closes in for the kill.

A muffled shriek
Frightens the valley
With a wavering echo.
The loud flapping
Of death pummels up air
Against gravity and grit.
A big bird flies away
With mortality's soft bundle
In a crushing grip.

The wind sighs softly
Through the trees
As peace returns.
And the sun plays
Hide and seek
With dappled shadows
On silent ground.

Bushland Folk

One day, not so very long ago
A childhood memory returned to me
As I meandered through a seaside garden
While the sun leaned lazy over in the west.

Dry tussocks of beach grass
Create paths here and there.
A child's wild garden, a dreamtime,
Of getting lost and found again.

Once I played under a grand tree like this…
It's sunken boughs and shadowed light
Remind me of those childish games.
Solace to keep a lonely heart at bay.

This hushed place belongs to pademelons
A secret clearing a meeting place, perhaps?
Where tunnels under leafy tresses
Lead to bushy trails and hidden cosy dens.

I hear dull thuds of furry feet retreat
Over spongy soil and softly littered leaves
As I, a stranger to a sanctuary
Intrude upon their peaceful games.

A green rosella and his wife
Take a muddy bath in evening puddles.
A carefree moment, intimate playful duet.
As water trickles, flicking through dusty feathers.

A yellow-tailed black cockatoo
Croons to his mate like a crying baby.
And she, lying hidden, replies
With an equally tuneless song, of love perhaps…

But as the sun sinks down to rest
I return to my abode,
And leave behind that quiet place
To its hidden watchful owners.

The bushland folk.

Hold on!

Hold on! Hold on.

Swim like the rolling beavers
As the water shelves away to the deep
And the thin green line of hope
Grows taut to the snapping point.

But beavers can dive deep
With certain memory of the door
To their home in the riverbank.
Where babies sleep in dark hidden slumber.

Holding on! Holding on.

As the green line grows thinner
The wish to give up grows stronger.
'But you can't give in! You can't give in.'
The small cry cries, as it bubbles to your lips.

Legs grow weary, tired of swimming
And the mind disassembles into shattered points
Under the heavy wave as it finally flips.
There is breath again and a change of direction.

Hold on to them! Hold on to them.

As the babies sleep with their fears and tears
And their dreams in the warm family heart.
With no notion of a care worn parent's love.
And the meaning of the thin green line.

Hold on!… Holding on…

To the thin green line of hope.

Fish in the wrong sea

The little fish looked at me sadly and said,

'I think I'm a fish in the wrong sea.
Caught under the ice floes of the frozen North Pole.
My home is so far away in the balmy Indian Ocean.

Poor me.

But I think there is a part of me that refuses to change.
Perhaps metamorphosis is not in my genes?

Poor me.

I'm really a fish living my life in a small fish tank.
But someone once read me a story about my lost ocean.
And that's where I long to be.

Poor me.

Perhaps they shouldn't have read me that story.

Poor me!'

Ode to the Rambling House

We go together into the old rambling house.
You find a room at the back unnoticed before,
And you open the door.

An unexplored country is found.
And water seeps out of the stream
That had always been, flowing.

You add a stain or colour,
Yes, colours like paint from your pallet.
They flow and they mingle.

Old memories like black and white movies
Were devoid of sound.
Now they have feelings, emotions of all colours.

Despite years of destruction flowers still bloom
In these quiet meadows and backwaters.
Secret hiding places in your landscape.

Truth and freedom are the prisoners you read about.
They have stood still, hidden for safe keeping.
Frozen in drab clothing, invisible inside your house.

They have waited in silence for years
To be disinterred by you from the dungeons of suffering.
And to re-enter the halls of delight.

Blown Away

The scattering
And tumbling of leaves.
Pages falling from a book
Thoughts slowly unhinging.
Hanging loosely down.

Loss of time.

Clouds like flecked wisps
Blown carelessly
Against a big blue void.
Birds flung chaotically around
In the grey flurry of a winged storm.

Blown away.

Ringing ears, faint echoes
Hollow footfalls,
Slamming doors
Whirring contorted confusion.

Loss of time.

Arrival of a bombshell
Exploding thunder
And lightning strikes.
Torture in an aching head.

Blown away.

Between the lines

What lies between the lines?

Vast spaces of things unsaid.

Thoughts that have no shape

Dreams that have no voices.

What a different world it would be

If we spoke in wordless songs

Instead of flying endlessly around

Somewhere inside our heads.

Unpredictable Weather

Every day every hour
The weather changes here inside my head.

Yesterday's weather.

There was a frenzied storm
A torrential downpour of buffeted feelings
Scattering like hail damage.
Leaves battered stamped to the ground.
Spring blossoms beaten up
Drooping sadly.
Icy winds whip up from a frozen north.
Soughing mournfully
Over rocks, through cracks.
Floods of hot tears drown torn up oaks.
Lightning and thunder
Electrify dangerous purple skies.

Today's weather.

It is drizzling, complaining, whining.
Snaggy clouds drag up from a grey horizon.
The day winds down.
Becomes restricted into whingeing
Fidgety shadows.
The sun slips into a pillowed veil
Of grumpy headaches.

Tomorrow's weather.

It will be mellow yellow
Horizons crystal clear.
Never is the laughing air more bright, more light,
Than after days of rain.
Sunbeams shaft dizzily over glinting seas.
Slide smilingly above drifting meadows.
Roll languidly around forested gullies.
Shimmy lazily on green hills.
Country gardens delight with rich heavy smells
Of musty moist earth,
Freshly mown grass
And thickly scented dancing summer flowers.

I can never predict the weather
Here inside my head.

February in Sydney

Summers end bursts
Into a frenzied bubble
Of volcanic heat.

Sudden hailstones
The size of golf balls
Reduce trees
To lightly leaved shadows
Of their former selves.

The icy stones
And whipped greenery
Lie in crunchy circles
On pitted ground
As we stumble around
Over shocked grass
In the aftermath.

February is a hard month
When there is a stir-crazy sense
Of melting maceration in the brain.
Of migrainous sweaty nightmares
And infra-red twilights.
Stifling humidity
Under muffled woollen clouds.

And all the languid while
Your fish swim quietly in their tank,
Light and breezy
Through liquid forests,
In a vastly silent underworld.

The Pointless Point

The pointless point
Is a place of dark suspicions
That shadow a soul's departure.
Like spattered paint strokes
On paper that only make sense
When it comes
To thoughts of chaos.

A grieving heart
And trapped soul lie there
In the place of mud.
This point is returned to,
Time and time again
Endlessly repeating
The poisoned mantra
Of falling out of Mondays
Into its tattered self.

And all that has ever been seen
Or felt in that place of self
Are the tough scars
Of an earthly existence.
And from there the lines
Of past and future
Extend infinitely
In all directions.
Relentlessly.

The carapace of life's trauma
Takes its toll
On a gentle poetic soul
Who is fragile
Like a battered butterfly.
But is all thoughtlessness
And naivety about
The vicissitudes of the world.

The depth of viciousness
Even now is not apparent,
Still mantled dispassionately
In dark corners of neglect.
Many journeys have ended in untruths.
But is that good enough for one lifetime?

And what is the point?

Fun at the Very Expensive Sydney Hotel

We stay at the Hotel.
The Very Expensive Sydney Hotel.
We arrive late
And it is raining lightly outside.

We are tired
And we want to sit alone
At dinner.
But we must sit with others
And make small talk.
It continues to rain outside
And it is very noisy inside.

The meal takes hours to come
The order is wrong
But the soup,
When it eventually comes,
Is very good.
But that is all
There is to eat
So it seems.
And the wine
Keeps flowing like the rain.

Our eyes grow heavy
Neck muscles clench up
Jaws ache.
The room starts to echo
The rain falls steadily, heavily.

There is an upset
A sudden tumble
From a chair
Pins and needles in hands
And a sore bottom.
How embarrassing!
And the rain falls heedlessly.

An angry exit
Shocked abandonment
Followed by a surprise return.
We feel drunk.
Where on earth is the food or the chef?
A shaky apologetic waiter kneels.
Heavens!
But by now the rain is overflowing.

We wait a few more minutes
But soon it's far too late
So we finally leave
And order the remains of a meal
To our room.
The rain steams up the windows.

The air is damp and heavy.
Finally we eat and then sleep
Distantly from each other,
Crestfallen.
In a huge bed.
The rain falls ceaselessly
All night.

Fun at the Very Expensive Sydney Hotel!

African Tapestry

Many faces, Young faces, Old faces,
Beautiful faces, Chiselled faces,
Handsome faces, Ruined faces.

Rags, Tin shacks, Poverty,
Thrown shoes, Old shoes,
Big shoes. Shabby trousers,
Short trousers, Torn trousers.

Tiny boy, Big mother, Tired mother,
Thin children, Toothless woman,
Beggars, Beggar children,
Beggar boy, Beggar toddlers,
Homelessness, Street kids.

Felt hurt, Soul cut,
Heartbreak, Soft pleas, Sad eyes,
Plaintive voices, Hard guilt.

Skin and bones, Scars, Tattoos,
Amputations, Lamentations,
Vitiligo, Desperation.

Rastafarian hairstyles, Plaits, Hats,
Odd fashion, Bright fashion, Bold colours,
Market stalls, Weary vendors, Street cleaners.

White smile, Quick wit, Song burst, Dance,
Drums, Jazz, Laugh, Warm hello, Forgetfulness,
Colour, Voodoo art, Tribalism.

Overwhelmed, Yearning, Your love,
Holding hands, Warm hugs, My dove,
Your friends, Sad news, Your tears,
Secrets, Your sweetness, Strange dreams.

The Harmless Man

Despair lives
As abject horror
Behind the haunted eyes
Of a man in rags
Who holds up his armless arms
To my tinted window.

Please buy my wares
Throw me your pennies
I want to live another day.

You don't know
That I am beaten.
And how I have fallen
Through all the layers
Of poverty and deprivation.

The shame of abject destitution
Is written as furrowed scars
In my weathered face.

You only have to look
To see that I am broken
Beyond trauma.
I live a tiny buried life
Somewhere inside my head.

I cannot imagine your life
Of luxury and privilege
Behind the shielded chrome.
And you cannot imagine mine.

I wonder, as I gaze
Across the gulf between us.
What kind of human animal
Bequeaths such suffering
To this abandoned man?

I believe it is you and I.

Life at Traffic Lights

I wonder who she is?
The young woman
In a straw hat
Seated in the dusty heat
With a small boy at her side,
On the hard pavement of life.

I wonder for whom
They wait
And what brave stories
She tells him
As the steel rimmed
Wheels of wealth flash by.

Do they wait
For the men
In leather shoes
Gold necklaces
And rings, that step
Anonymously
From their cars of chrome?

And what does she suffer
As they move inside
The black sedan
Of darkness and pain?
All for bread on the table
And in the name
Of bitter survival.

A Painful Etching

Extreme heat twists necks in a knot.
Light-headedness sets in
And illness creeps along
In a hot capsule.
As the destitute old man
Begs and bows
Bows and scrapes
Grimaces and bobs.
Over and over at the lights.

A burst to scream
Silently arises.
Please stop!
For God's sake!
It's long over.
It is OK now
Or is it? No it's not.
Just forgive me then. Please!

Midday is a full-time headache.
Achingly beautiful blue
As awful shacks fly by.
Dregs of humanity
Bottoming out my intense shame.
As it still putrefies
Your darkened world.
Old scars under sunburnt skin
That can't be washed away.

Funeral has gone by
Disowned, without telling.
And overlooked flowers
Are unborn and won't be buried.
Deep hurt covers
Quickly
Like a body alone in its coffin.
Her light glows brightly in my head.
Then dies
With a popping sound.
Goodbye dearest lonely.

Old aggression
Still thrashes about
In a hospital
Of chaotic death throes.
Unlike her delicate
Arrangements
Carefully written long ago
When no one was about.
No kin to shed tears
Over her remains.
A long dry winter
As old age withers into death.
In spite of feuds
She quietly waits
For the long slumber
With mother interred.
Nothing left behind, just tidy.

And ashes of your kin
Forever young.
Unfinished.
Hard closure for those who slept
Then twisted the wheel.
And she was flung
Suddenly, to death.
It is forgiven unforgetfulness
In spite of the wind change.
Howling her dust to earthly corners.

So many threads
Converge today
As it turns down cold.
And the mountain loses itself
In a cloudy shroud
As we look at each other.
So much older
Staring at our crows feet
And whiskers.

What would she say
If she saw you today over coffee?
Bobbing and bowing
Grimacing and scraping
Begging forgiveness.
Would she laugh
Lightheartedly.
Or burst out screaming to stop?

Lives lived since her passing
Have suffered
A lifetime of pain
In the blink of her going.
Grief etches its lines
Like deep ravines
On the faces of those left behind.

Incongruity

The pulsating heart of Africa
Heralds another glorious pink dawn
With the birth of fragile birdsong.
Softly cooing doves,
Complaints from a cuckoo bird.
The loud 'ha-di-da' of an ibis.

But peacock cries are muffled
By police cars that blare
Accusing macho horns.
And sirens chase
The unlucky despair of men
Excluded by electrified walls
From the exquisitely rich,
Who hide and skulk
In manicured gardens.

A bird oranges in the grey shadows
Of the warming yellow light.
And it's fluted notes tread quietly
Over an old mans much loved farm.
A bygone era of high teas,
Tennis, hen house and vegetable patch.

Paradise once, to rowdy boys
A haven on the Highveld.
The garden now crumbling quietly
In on itself, inside a tangle of fences,
Thirsty trees, brown calves, dead grass.

New city dust blows in as old colonial ways
Slink out and plunge headlong
Onto the highways of gaudy skyscrapers.
Streetscapes for the rich and famous
Yet abject poverty abounds.
Hungry eyes beseech
Sealed car doors and averted hearts.

Road gangs crack hot asphalt
And hear their hungry babies cry.
While someone's wife
Remains a hapless silent maid
In uniformed servitude.
And a small entitled child
In the kitchen of endless kindnesses
Has not yet learnt to say, 'Thank you.'

Geese hiss greedily for food
In dusky afternoon light.
Guinea fowls hunch and cry alarm.
A wild bunny from nowhere
Incongruously loves a dog.
They crouch and silently note
Mandela's fading dream
Of freedom and democracy
In this bountiful beautiful land.

The prickly conscience of frog song
Startles in a choked up dam
Of bitter political disappointments.
And is heard from the steps of the farmhouse
To the new democratic parliaments
Of corruption and despair.

The broiling blood of the setting red sun
Ushers in rustlings and birdsong at twilight.
As a mantle of hopelessness
Now surrenders to the stifled cries of sorrow
And to another heavy nightfall
In this darkening African land.

Camp Figtree

A baboon barks
On waking hills.
Eaves creak in warming light.
Bees hum busy tunes.

A lone fly escapes
The waking tin house.
That sways on spindly poles
Over a ravine
With each gentle step.

A cool breeze whispers
Through an open door
Ruffling mosquito nets.

Distant gunshots ricochet
Down winding valleys
Coiling like snake spits.

Bush mantles rolling hills
And green trees shade
The brown cow
Who moos her solitary pleasure
In dappled pastures
Far below.

Distant cliffs jut up
To scratch the sky.
And hide an animal kingdom
That lies beyond
Human experience.

Birds warble songs
Of breathless delight.
Only to fling themselves
Kamikaze style
Off the veranda.
And swoop dizzily down
Over the yawning abyss.

Softly the morning breeze
Caresses greying hair
And kisses wiser eyes.
As the new day settles itself
Into an ancient African rhythm.

The Goodbye Tale

The going goodbye
Is something
That I see in your face fall.
Your sad eyes can't smile any more
And I follow with mine.

Please don't feel sad.
I cannot mend
The widening crack between us.
Hastily we speed,
Expediently
To our other worlds also in full moon.

The prospective future without you
Follows the past that you were present in.
It has a rapid diminishing, vanishing point
Called forgetfulness.
No more grasping at old hopes
Of happy ever after.
Sadness itself is swept away by endless tides.

Before our going, the brown dove's song
Drowned out thought.
Except crying and crying to use the key
For the place of ashes.
Caught sunbeams in the camera lens
Told the Goodbye Tale
Of where she lies in rest.
But nothing's left.

In memory
Sounds of water
Trickle through my ears.
Faded imagery of gnarled trunks,
A green sight for my eyes.
Dusty bone and stones,
A dryness in my mouth and nose.
And small wells of parched grief
Still follow us around
For years like lost children.
In your sad eyes,
I see the dove, stream, trees, ashes, key
And deep wells of wandering orphans.

They are the keepers of the Goodbye Tale.

The Frogs Dream

At the bottom of a muddy pond
A little green frog

Peers out
From under his stone.
He longs to swim up
To the surface
Of the water.
To touch the sky.

He longs to breathe
In the silky night air
And gaze at the stars.
To dream
Himself
Into that butterfly
Or a bee.
To fly like that swan,
Below the halo of the moon.

He longs to feel
The morning sunlight
Of pure joy

Warming his brave heart.
Just for a day.
And he longs to know

That all will be well
In his little world.

That's all.

Images of Tsunamis and Bubbles

Jumping on stepping stones you cross over the River of Life.
That like a tsunami threatens to engulf you with fear.

But each island is a refuge of happy memories amidst the raging foam.
Pushing back for a moment, threats of painful annihilation.

The bubbles of foam capture your thoughts.
Their thickness a hair's breadth, between existence or not.

A different layer from the rigid dome
That once allowed you to disappear.

The membrane you speak of today is fragile, transient, permeable.
Yet has a substantial quality.

Like new life.

A newborn covered inside his sac of connections.
And swimming in his own Sea of Tranquillity.

You thought you would die at birth but you didn't.
And here you are.

The River of Life carries the silt of fertility downstream to the valleys,
In spite of its destructive ways.

Yesterday you were afraid and thought your voice
Would drown at the bottom of a well.

Today you dropped in a stone.
You listened in silence and heard a faint echo.

A cry.

Someone wants to be born.

Someone wants to play bubbles.

Disturbances

There's a disturbance in the pool of emotion.
A ripple.
A shadow.
The flutter of wings.
A magpie's swoop to the back of the head.
What is it that has been forgotten?
Disremembered?

There is an alarm ringing.
Faraway down a well.
Muffled sighs through trees.
Faint moans down valleys.
Arctic winds whispering over icy mountains.

Who is the caller?

Where are they calling from?

Should I listen?

What should I say in reply?

Long Lost, Last Deeplove

We all fall into the pit of despair
Alone,
You know.
But…
Perhaps if you already know that,
Then I'm not alone.

But…

Don't I count?
Don't I have in place in your mind?
Don't I Exist?

I think that I'm misunderstood,
I can't be heard.
It is too much to ask of you.
Who has been so gentle,
So kind.

It is truly enough.
And the rest of what's left,
I will bear alone.

Over the edge the fall begins.
I feel lost again

And so alone.

Is long lost, last Deeplove
There to save me?
Perhaps not.
But it's the last long thought,
Of Deeplove,

That saves me from myself.

The Thing in Itself

You wait in a timeless nowhere place
To discover what will be revealed.
Your mind is the object.
It is what it is.
The thing in itself.

But you just want to be.
To exist in limbo.
Suspended animation.
Frozen in a carapace.
No past, no future, no time.

Life is a nuisance
And nibbles at your ankles
Like a hungry dog.
And your existence
Becomes the fog
Around living trees
And moisture on leaves.
Yet you still live on the fringes.

Go into your house.
Close windows and doors.
Open doors inside,
To rooms you locked long ago.
To rooms you have never opened.

In that inside space
You will find your map
And you will find your compass.
Your mind is the object
You have been given.

It is what it is.
The thing in itself.

A Force of Nature

So! Crying memories
Are a force of nature.

Long forgotten sad memories
Hide abandoned
In this old house.
Some years have passed
And a forest
That has lain buried
Reawakens.

Slowly, but surely
Saplings push upwards
Through flagstones.
Across floorboards.
Crisscross walls
Pretty much everything.
To reach the light.

The house becomes
An unnecessary thing
Tossed aside
In the burgeoning jungle.
Silently crumbling
Involuting. Lost.
A ghost without tears.

Other crying memories
Settle like ash seeds
Hidden lightly in the soil.

Waiting for spring.
Until the thing,
The false belief,
The habitual way of being
Falls away.
Collapses into nothing.

Then life slowly,
Steadily
Without beckoning returns.
To cry, to feel sad.
To restore the mind
Knowingly.
So you see
Crying memories are like that.
A force of nature.

Below 432 Hertz*

Below 432 Hertz
Piano music vibrates in the heart.

Muffled awakening.
Water falling,
Flowing.
Images rippling in shadows.
Dappled light playing like a faded movie.

Childhood dreams,
Of running lightly looking back.
Waving, smiling,
To someone just out of sight.
Yearning,
To return and start over.

Unspoken sounds
Sing, swing
Swirl and resonate
With some kind of truth.
Trying to pull it altogether.

Tears trickle,
Dizzy,
Twirling,
Whirling dervishes.
Gushing sounds tickle ears
Like string instruments.

Soaring in mid-flight, echoing a full life.

The music vanishes.
Concert over.

* Inspired by musician Joep Beving and his piano composition titled *432*.

Mass Extinctions

Possums snarl and grunt desires
As they chase across the rooftops.

Flying foxes squawk and tussle passionately
In palm trees.

The tawny frog mouth owl serenades his mate
Quietly, with a song. 'Woo woo.'

Crickets crick, click and creak their violins.
Frogs croak hopeful melodies in muddy hollows.

The moon hangs like a silent witness in the sky
And all the while soft shadows glide and slide.

Whispering mist tumbles quietly down the hillside.
Slipping over fields, sighing through the bush

Flowing into empty streets.
Blanketing the old world in silvery dew.

All seems well in nature's velvet fantasy.
But humanity sleeps restless in its bed.

And dreams the sleepless dreams
Of mass extinctions.

For the last male northern white rhino is dead.

Who's next?

Free Fall

This morning
It feels like the world is in free fall.
The insects and birds are silent.
Have they gone?

There's a heavy mist in the garden
Enveloping everything.
Are the plants
Giving up their water
Because the rain
Has forgotten how to rain?

Stepping outside
From inside my head
I recall another distant foggy morning.
Where sounds echoed.
Hollow.
As if standing in a cathedral.
A breath, shuffle, movement.
All magnified, clear, pure.
Each sound born and heard
For the first time,
With the shut down of sunlight.
Vision obscured by mist.

Somewhere else,
A raucous street up ends itself
In a blaze of carcinogenic light.
Even as traffic whizzes by
Still yelling it's smoky tunes.
A massive din as it disappears
Down the road towards extinction.
Like pebbles
Racketing down a chute.

Silence descends in my head.
And hearing can hear itself think again.
The last footsteps retreat
Behind a slammed door.
As if the last human left standing
In the world,
Has anonymous feet…

Climate change is in free fall.

Farewell Messages

An ancient flame is flickering down the hall.
A moonbeam falls by chance across my bed.
I hear your gentle voice beckoning me to come soon.
Inside my sleepless head.

I shall bring our lighted candle to your side
And we'll dance to the lunacy of happenstance.
That you gave birth to me so long ago
When all the lights went out and thunder roiled.

And when the flame gutters in the faded cradle
You will sigh your last breath of sweet caresses.
A quiet spirit shall leave your maternal abode
And bid farewell to children one and all.

The Gaps

Sadness lies between the gaps,
Between our words.
Between our worlds.
Between the autumn leaves
Over here and over there.
Where you keep watch
At the window
For spring buds.

Sadness lies in the gap
Between our farewell.
Your smile.
The moment of departure.
And the many moments just after…

A sad sprite lives
Between the gaps.
And feels the hardship of farewells
But will not remember them.

Unlike the other you
Who writes the history book
Of words.
Of your life into memory.

Sadness is the sprite
In the gaps.

But your pages
Are forever turning.
As you live your busy life
In blocks of blocking time.
That block out sadness
And obliterate the gaps
In between.

And so.

Sadness and our words
Fall between the gaps
And into forgetfulness.

Another Day in Finality

The crow caws out a warning with all his strength
To the sun-soaked morning.
From high atop the chimney stack he flies away.
Black.
Against a blue moon,
Opalescent through the treetops.

Spring flowers brighten a vase jauntily.
Then fade.
Sunlight glances into a room
Of ever hopeful desperations.
Warming old bones that wither away
Anyway.
Quietly.
To a greater silence.

We drive along the coast road.
Sea mist billows up and over crumbling cliffs.
Hiding steel blue water.
Motionless in the bay.
Slack as a millpond with the tide gone out.

Walkers disappear like spirits swallowed whole.
And then reappear
Hovering.
Uncannily.
Out of the creeping sea fog.
That streams like clammy fingers over rooftops.

There's a deep pervasive smell of clustered hyacinths.
Abundant.
Intoxicating.
In cultured Castle flower beds.
Seeping rain, light as fairy tears on upturned faces.
A patch of blue sky and an inquisitive child.

But there's always sadness
Drawing us back to the old stone house.
A silent granite witness
To the black crow,
Creeping fog,
Faded flowers and withered bones.
All waiting for one thing to come.

To pass.

Walking in the Park

There is no kindness in words.
The cold landscape is written within us
In winters colours.
Sapped of strength.
Coated folks in a park are bright dots
Of hope, moving slowly.
But they too, fade softly into pale green meadows.

There is no forgiveness,
No forgetting.
The winters harshness
And recent super storms
Have scoured the fertile soil
And left behind acres of polluted mud.
The spring harvest lies in ruins.

There is no will to understand
What lives between the wrecked branches
Of ancient trees.
They regret finding themselves
Clawing, helpless and hopeless,
At the fearful future of desecrated forests.
And climate change.

I believe that I want to understand
I want forgiveness.
And I want to be kind.
Spring flowers stand up fearlessly
Below the mossy gnarled trunks.
Against the grey dirt, and leaking sky.
Like determined beacons of hope.

We should leave behind our rancour,
Our wounds, our collective guilt.
But the landscape is folding up.
Collapsing in on itself.
Crushing out dank air and seeping colour
As the fog descends.
Eternity is the extinguishing of everything.

All we can do is make peace, now.
And hope for summer to burst through again.
Before it's too late.

Water

It feels womb-like
Inside my room.
Listening to rain.
Water moving all around an outer skin.
Stone walls fade
To rocking boat.
A cradle.

Comfort
Is the knowledge
That Nature has been kind enough
To hold me in her arms.
Rocking me gently on life's ocean.

So please be kind to one
Who waits by the window.
Light as a feather
Fragile as a shell.
Waiting for spring rain to fall
Once more
On a distant shore.

She waits for thee
To bring her home again.
And embrace her
Lovingly,
Without terror.
Safe in the harbour of deepest slumber
And final resignations.

Water Colours

Water colours
Fade to mist.
A disquieted sprite
Wanders like a lost waif
Among bare trees.

Emotions tangle
In black branches.
Plastic bags snag like flowers
After a massive storm.

Disconnected
From pure form
In a day of impossible living.
Torn by passion,
Water colours
Run in all directions.

The gentle symphony
Of morning birds
Doesn't comfort
This watery world.

The doves soft cooing
Echoes
Through a wood
Of wasted consolations.

Reality injures
The dream colours
And washes out
Vibrant hues.

Being real
Cannot be glimpsed
Through a fog
Of injury and escape,
Without disconnecting the heart.

But it is here now.
In all its brutal colours.

Selective Memories

Memories are selective.
And at the end
I want to remember you
In an idyllic way.
From here.

In the beginning
There was a dream
Of a beatific spirit.
Pure form.
Gentle presence.
I felt loved, wholly.

Then I fell into fear.
A deep hunger to be loved.
Was it me who loved you alone?
Was it you who loved me?
Was it just a wistful dream?

Did we find each other?
Did we weep together?
Did you weep for me?
Or was I loving, weeping
And frightened alone?
Were you loving, weeping
And frightened alone?

I'm wishing love
Into existence,
Now.

Generosity is called love.
I want to love you from here.
Generously.
I have always loved you,
But not always generously.

Can we find each other now?
From here?
At the end?

Ordinary Things

We did ordinary things.
We looked at her clothes
While he fell asleep in the chair.

She stroked old fur coats.
Tried on a hat, a scarf.
He woke and laughed
She smiled.
And I took photos.

We sorted the jewellery.
Looked at medallions.
Rosary beads.
Decided who should get what.

She worried about a card
Misplaced.
We searched bags.
Grew weary
And finally forgetful.

There was comfort
In the ordinariness
Of doing things.
On our last days

Together.

Humming

Occasionally

There can be a kind of hum.
A deep rich vibration of feelings.
Between parents and their children.

We sat together.
In the sunshine.

Quietly.

Chatting.

Smiling.

For one brief moment
The universe hummed.

I was home.

Dear Old Soul

She won't last long
Dear old soul.
Grief floods my heart to think it.
That we
Shall soon be left alone
This side of the Great Divide.

It really is too late
To take one last walk with her,
In wild abandoned late summer garden.
Where heavy flowers grow giddily
In final honeyed profusion.

My mother
No longer ventures
Down worn-out garden paths.
Nor sits in floral abundance
Below the redwood tree.

Listening to the rampant birdsong in her heart.

Angel Wings

You are so weak.
You can hardly speak.
You will leave soon.

Long ago
When you spoke
Quietly
From the sky
The waters
Broke their banks
And life began.
But now
Your life is ebbing
As I speak.

Sometimes
Your voice
Is still here
In my ear.
An echo
In my heart.
And mine in yours.

Do we hold each other
Once more
Before you fall?

Or do we miss
And fall
Interminably
Apart?
Just out of reach.
Out of time.

Like feathers,
Scattered
Thoughtlessly.
From angel wings.
Towards unfathomable grief.

Ferryman from the River Styx

Even now she won't go.

As the evening languishes into dusk
And blue blushes to a rose pink
Twilight.
And the orange evening
Slants across the floor through an open door
And fretful shadows fade to a yellow
That overflows to deeper shades of grey that creep
Slowly through mote laden air.

And even now she says there are things to do. To finish.

A listening presence pauses its advances
And the desire to scoop her up and away
And is led astray.
Smitten by an assault on senses
As floral perfume wafts
Its hefty pungent scent.
On lighter breezes
Through open windows
Stirring curtains slightly in the gloaming.

A familiar yet ephemeral voice
Whispers in her ear to enfold herself
In his intoxicating embraces
And float away on life's river.

And even now she hesitates.

Dark stands of nearby trees exhale
A watery mist of grieving tears
Around glistening trunks.
And sunset embers hiss and sizzle
Dissolving to a quiet mournful dampness
In the silent cloistered garden.

The moment passes by with a sigh
As scatterings of leaves
Scuttle noisily.
And rattling breath
Sags out of a dying day.

And even now at nightfall she will not go.

The gate latch clicks
And the ferryman departs alone.

Rose Water

for Mother

Tawny light pink
Silky petals.
Thick and glossy
Cling steadfastly together.
To life.

Honeyed perfume.
Old world fragrance
Delicately alluring.
Lingers in the twilight
Of a humid evening.

The air is moist, heavy.
Drenched with yellow light
And the potent weight of rain.
An unfallen evening dew.

Petals scatter suddenly,
Flurry all around.
Withered to the ground.

The rose has gently faded.
But in my memory
A sweet scent still remains.
Laden with rose water.

Not Ever

I'll always be running to catch up with you
Forever…forever

I'll never be able to reach you
Never…not ever

I'll always be wanting to hold you
Wanting to hold you

I'll never be able to touch you
Touch you

I'll not be with you any more
Not ever.

Green sky

for J.B.

Out in your boat
On the bay
One day
With your child from the wild
The green clouds gathered
And threatened
To take you away.
Faraway.
But you both made it home
To shore,
Once more.

Out in your boat
All alone today
The green sky took you
Away.
Far faraway.
You won't make it home
To shore
Any more.

Dear You

You laugh out loud with the songbirds
I'll miss that.

You smile easily as your voice tips into mirth.
I'll miss that.

There is music around every word.
I'll miss that.

Passion bubbles like a stream from your heart
I'll miss that.

You are a great unifier of people.
I'll miss that.

You feed us food but you also feed our souls.
Already I miss all of that about you.

Come back soon.

In the moment

Listening to expectant silence
In the moment
As feet touch squeaky sand
And warm breezes caress the air.
Flapping gently like wings around boulders.
The quiet lap of waves shift shingle
And drifts out to green translucent water
That flows like molten glass against black rocks
That jag against a powder blue sky.

Silence under sound is heard
In the moment
When waves bubble up with laughter
Chasing, circling in surprise.
A deep boom thuds further on
As white horses curve over
And leap headlong up the beach
Spraying us with salty fingers of delight.
And we walk along
Smilingly as if in Eden

Listening to expectant silence
In the moment
On a sun drenched pier
Our shadows ripple over hazy shallows
Carving tracks, walking on water.
Where baby fish teem under pylons
And mussels harvest their delicacies.
Where oystercatchers run in ruffled pairs
Tripping lightly ahead.
Swooping back and trotting away again.

Silence under sound is heard
In the moment
As pelicans soar.
Majestic flying boats
Patrolling choppy waterways
That wisp into wind blown peaks.
Yachts tinkle, twinkle
Dancing, swaying on moorings.
Waiting for recreational crews
To return to summer havens of play
In the shimmering bay.
And we walk along
Smilingly as if in Eden.

Thanking God

While I was thanking God,
If there is a God to be thanked
For giving me life
And continuing to give me life,
A small quiet voice could be heard
In my head, clear as a crystal bell.

'So OK, why don't you go
And live a peaceful useful life now?
Try to be happy and content.
You have no way of knowing
What lies ahead,
And the past only confuses you.
Be satisfied with what you have now
And what you don't have
And may never have.

When you are happy,
I am more happy,
And I am less happy than you.
When you are sad,
I am more sad
And I am less sad than you.
When you are angry, guilty or afraid
I feel all that you feel both more and less.

I know everything that there is to know
Yet I know nothing.
I am all things,
I am also nothing.
I am everywhere and nowhere.

And even though you may think,
After what I have said to you
That you are unimportant and insignificant,
You are very important to me
Just like every living thing
And every non-living thing.

So now that you know
Who and what you are to me
And who and what you ought to be for you,
Go and live a peaceful useful life
So that you can bear witness
To everything and nothing for us
And live a good life and die a good death… With me.'

The Muse Slumbers

The Muse lies quietly on her couch.
Still and strangely silent.

Tranquil under silky wraps

She has not raised her head for days.
But sleeps a peaceful slumber.

Her door is closed

No sound is heard.
No calls returned

No songs exchanged.
No poems born.

Enchantment has been put away.
Inspiration interrupted.

The pen lies fallow on the page.
A canvas untouched in its frame.

The room is now an empty field

The curtains drawn against the light.

The poet has finally left her chair
And gone on a long vacation.

The Blackbird

I sit.

My feet in the cool water,
While nature returns
To a quiet clearing in my mind.
The source of the spirit lulls me.
There is no din
But the sublime peace
Of a living moment.

I am a great bird.
A being with black feathers
Shrouded in the shadow
Of early morning mystery.
I dip my talons
Into the pool
Of deepest thoughts.
My shoulders hold the weight
Of ages past.
My wings the flight
To an endless future.

My thoughts hold the secrets
Of the light within.
I am still and rested.
And the songs you sing me
Tinkle at the close of day
In my memory,
And forever in my dreams.

www.ingramcontent.com/pod-product-compliance
Lightning Source LLC
Chambersburg PA
CBHW070939080526
44589CB00013B/1572